A BIRTH AWAY FROM HOME

A Birth Away from Home

NICK THOMAS

Convivial Books

Introduction

The English Reformed Church is not a denomination, as the name seems to suggest, but a building and a community in the centre of Amsterdam. The city's worthies offered this large and beautiful church for the use of English-speaking Christians in 1607, and it is now part of the Church of Scotland, serving a membership of 400 people from all over the world, including many native Dutch who enjoy its ecumenical churchmanship, and worship there happily in their fluent English.

When my wife and I moved from London to Amsterdam with our two small children in 2011, it was here that we found a spiritual home and most of our new friends. In due course my wife joined the rota for running the crèche, and after four years I became a lay preacher and then a member of Consistory, the governing committee of the church; whereupon the American colleague who had been organising the annual Nativity play, using a traditional format, announced that she was returning to the US. I had been foolish enough to mention that I had experience in theatre, as both playwright and director, and so naturally I was now, as she put it with a grin, 'It'.

I didn't want to be 'It' at all. Though I delighted in the company of my own children, as a child myself I had loathed all my contemporaries for the malodorous barbarians they were. And even in middle age I felt an irrational fear that the members of our Sunday School - the pool of talent, up to 12 years old, on which I must draw - would conspire to bully me.

There were other deterrents. Ours was a 'gathered' congregation, of people who commuted from the edge of the city and beyond to meet for worship at 10.30 on a Sunday morning, and so individual attendance could be erratic. Continuity, from one year to the next, was patchy, with so many ex-pat families at the mercy of multinational employers. We had no parish, let alone an associated primary school, which meant that rehearsals had to be organised around the promises of parents to deliver their brood into my care over a series of Sundays before the performance. The play was an interlude during a regular service, which meant performing in the aisle and before the table (as Presbyterians call the Altar), to an audience of about 250; but we only had two microphones, one fixed in the pulpit and the other on a cable, detachable from the lectern used for reading the lessons. Parents had to make sure the children learnt their lines at home. And, of course, the children themselves had to want to take part in the play. This last was by no means a given. Some thought they were too grown-up for this kind of thing, while the little tots were too scared, and the window between timorous diffidence and jaded swagger proved remarkably narrow.

But it had to be done, and, since it had to be done by me, I determined to do it with a difference, and work with what I had.

There is, to my mind, only one rule governing a Nativity play (apart from the avoidance of outright heresy), and that is that it must end with the Nativity scene. There must be a Mary, a Joseph, and a Baby Jesus (a doll in a blanket) in a crib. Ideally there are also children dressed up as shepherds and Magi, and a big golden star; if there are still some left over they can be animals and angels - the more the merrier, as long as they are all finally gathered in a dignified tableau of worship.

But, because everybody knows the story, there are many ways of getting to its climax.

In my first Advent as Nativity Play Supremo it was clear that I would always have to lean on an adult narrator reading from a script to propel the story, because there was no way the children were going to learn enough lines and stage directions in the time available to do it on their own. I just had to ensure that the action constantly illustrated the narration, with cues built into the text, so that all eyes remained on the juvenile cast.

But that year I had an asset at my disposal in the form of a boy of twelve, just about to leave Sunday School, who could be induced to take the male lead as long as it afforded him an outlet for his talent as a comic show-off. He was clearly unsuitable for Joseph - an Artful Dodger, not an Oliver, if you will - and so, taking my lead from T. S. Eliot, I decided to focus on the rich guys for a change, follow the Magi on their journey to Bethlehem, and play them for laughs, in a piece called *The Damascus Breakfast Club*. I was secretly hoping that the more conservative element in our congregation would be so appalled by this outrage that I would be politely relieved of my theatrical responsibilities forthwith. It didn't work. The crowd loved it.

The following year our wonderful Music Master, Richard Zook, approached me with a proposition. Since the Nativity Play was scheduled for a Choir Day (one Sunday in every four), would I mind incorporating his singers into the script? This was handy, because at the time I didn't have an idea in my head. And so came about *The Biggest Gig*, in which the Heavenly Choir is instructed by the Angel Gabriel to rehearse for a mysterious event that turns out to be the Nativity. Gabriel makes four appearances, and I intended him to be played by four different children, but when I canvassed the Sunday School that day they refused outright, with one exception, to take any speaking parts. The outlier was my own daughter, Zahra, who was thus catapulted to stardom, centre-stage in a solo turn. She was nine at the time. But the sight of her Gabriel camping it up in a knockabout cross-talk act with Richard as the Heavenly Choirmaster remains one of my favourite memories of our time in Amsterdam.

As the next Christmas loomed, Zahra, emboldened by fame and now taking drama classes, volunteered to write the play - then thought about it, and dumped it back on me. But at least she'd had an idea I could write up, albeit one that would probably only occur to a ten-year-old girl, about a mischievous lamb who ends up guiding the Magi and his own young shepherd to the Nativity. The innocent lamb is, of course, loaded with Christological significance, so even this lightweight bit of fun was theologically sound. But I thought it best not to spoil the moment by overthinking it. *Is This Your Sheep?* involved a small child in a white woolly jumper scampering around the church, to much good-natured laughter from the congregation, and a final speech from his shepherd so corny that even I, who had written the thing and rehearsed it to clockwork, got a tear in the eye at the end.

But when it was that time of year once again, we were preparing to move back to England, house-hunting and looking at schools. I would preach a couple more sermons before we left, and organise one last play, but as Christmas approached I found myself distracted by the imminence of change. Maybe that's why I decided to bow out by telling the story the old-fashioned way, but with a script in iambic pentameter to squeeze out some fresh poetic strokes. I had a bright, reliable

Joseph, and my son Will, now eight, relished his character cameo as the inn-keeper, but my only possible Mary (with Zahra determined to see out her tenure as Gabriel) was a sullen little madam who hadn't learnt even the minor parts she'd been given in previous plays. So, in *A Birth Away from Home*, the Blessed Virgin is a largely symbolic figure with only a couple of lines, a foil for the tormented husband at the centre of the drama.

All these plays can be adapted to suit any space, any size of audience. They take about fifteen minutes each to perform, but of course they can be padded out with carols, or trumpeters announcing the appearance of Gabriel, if you happen to have trumpeters at your disposal. There can be any number of sheep and stars and angels, street crowds, elaborate costumes, hand-made props and painted sets… Or just a clothes rack and a couple of blankets as backdrop to a cast of three doubling up parts in a classroom. The point is to involve children actively in Advent and Christmas, to make space for their own contribution, their own devotional effort. It's good for them. It was good for me, as well.

Nick Thomas
Oxford, 2023

The Damascus Breakfast Club

Dramatis personae
Narrator
Caspar, Balthazar, Melchior
Inn-keepers #1,2,3.
Mary
Joseph (non-speaking)
Choir

NARRATOR: Caspar was a very wise and wealthy man. By the time of his sixtieth birthday he had read every book in his enormous library many times. And all his life he had studied the sky, and he knew every star there was. But one fine evening he looked out of his window to the West, and jumped in surprise.

CASPAR: Hang on! That star wasn't there yesterday! I'm sure I've read about this somewhere!

NARRATOR: And he rushed to his library to hunt for the right book. He went through them all – history books, poetry books, cookery books, books about camels, books about pyramids, until finally:

CASPAR: Here it is! "The greatest king who ever lived will be born in the West, and a new star will rise to guide his true followers to his cradle, so that they might be the first to worship him!" Wow! This is exciting! I must go at once! Oh – I'd better take some gold.

NARRATOR: So he gathered up his maps and charts and a parcel of gold, loaded his camel, and set off into the night. He travelled for three days and nights, with no idea of how much further he had to go, so it was quite a relief when the star appeared to stop over the great city of Damascus. Caspar didn't know what to do next, but he was very hungry, so he went to the grandest café in town to get some breakfast. Breakfast had always been his favourite meal, and he was used to getting the best there was. When he'd finished, he looked around and saw two other men, with maps and charts a bit like his, one younger, the other **much** younger than himself.

CASPAR: Good morning, gentlemen! I am the famous wise man, Caspar. Are you by any chance here to worship a new-born king, the greatest there ever was or will be?

MELCHIOR: Yes, we are! I'm Melchior.

BALTHAZAR: And I'm Balthazar. We followed a star from our homes far away, and met here just now.

CASPAR: I hope you brought some gold. Kings like gold.

MELCHIOR: No. My charts told me that this king is the holy one of God, so I brought frankincense.

BALTHAZAR: And my books told me he will suffer for his people and for the whole world, so I brought some myrrh.

CASPAR: Mmm. I'm sure he'll like my gift the best. But how do we find him?

BALTHAZAR: The star! It led us here so that we could all meet and travel on together. But look! It's moving again!

CASPAR: We'd better get going.

NARRATOR: So they paid their bill and set off again, well fed and happy to have company, to follow the star wherever it led them.

CHOIR: WE THREE KINGS

NARRATOR: The time passed much more quickly now, and soon Caspar, Melchior and Balthazar reached the top of a hill, and saw that the star had stopped again, right over the little town of Bethlehem. So they hurried on through the gates.

MELCHIOR: What do we do now?

CASPAR: Easy! There's only one five star hotel in this place. He must be there. Leave this to me.

NARRATOR: So he went and knocked on the door.

FIRST INN-KEEPER: I'm terribly sorry, sir, I'm afraid we're fully booked tonight.

CASPAR: My friends and I are looking for a new-born baby. It's very important.

FIRST INN-KEEPER: There *was* a couple expecting a baby, but I had to send them away. I'm sorry sir.

MELCHIOR: Right, let's think about this. There are three of us, and he's three kinds of king all at once. Let's try the three star hotel.

NARRATOR: So he went and knocked on the door.

SECOND INN-KEEPER: Sorry! We're booked solid.

MELCHIOR: My friends and I are looking for a new-born baby. It's very important.

SECOND INN-KEEPER: There *were* some people expecting, but I had to send them away. Sorry!

NARRATOR: Then Balthazar said:

BALTHAZAR: What about the one star?

CASPAR: There are dozens of one star hotels!

MELCHIOR: We'll be searching all night!

BALTHAZAR: No, I mean the star that led us here. Look, it's over there.

MELCHIOR: But that's just a scruffy little inn!

CASPAR: And it's not even right over the inn. It's over the sheds at the back.

BALTHAZAR: Do you have any better ideas?

NARRATOR: So he went and knocked on the door.

THIRD INN-KEEPER: We're full!

BALTHAZAR: My friends and I are looking for a new-born baby. It's very important.

THIRD INN-KEEPER: Oh, them. They're in the sheds round the back.

CASPAR: Told you.

NARRATOR: So Balthazar, Melchior and Caspar picked their way through the mud and the rubbish bins to the door of the cow-shed. There they saw Mary and Joseph, and the baby Jesus asleep in the manger while some Shepherds knelt before him. And one by one they fell to their knees, laid down their gifts, and heard the angels singing around them.

CHOIR: AWAY IN A MANGER

NARRATOR: After that holy night the three wise men went back home the way they had come, and said goodbye where they had met, in Damascus. But they agreed to meet there for breakfast again every year, in memory of the most marvellous thing they would ever see. As time went on they began to hear stories of a young teacher who cast out demons and healed the sick, and then that he was the Son of God, and then of his suffering and death and resurrection. And soon they were meeting his followers in Damascus itself, for the Word was spreading everywhere.

Caspar was very old by then, and couldn't see the stars or read his books any more, but still he was content. And then, one year, a disciple of Jesus, passing through on his way to India, found the three friends in their café, and took them to be baptised. Caspar laughed with joy, then laughed at himself as he remembered how important he had thought his gold would be; and how, just before he left that cow-shed, with all its dung and dirt and its leaky, draughty roof, he had looked up at the one star still hanging above it and thought to himself:

CASPAR: One star for that? The breakfast must be amazing!

CHOIR: JOY TO THE WORLD

THE END

The Biggest Gig

Dramatis personae:
Narrator
Angel Gabriel
Heavenly Choir
Choir of Cherubs
Chorister #1
Chorister #2
Mary
Joseph
Magi
Shepherds
Star

The Heavenly Choir is rehearsing a 'Glory to God in the highest' chorus. After a few bars the choirmaster stops them.

CHOIRMASTER
OK, people, that's coming along nicely. Take five.

NARRATOR
The Heavenly Choir were very experienced. They had sung for God at the Creation, they had celebrated the rise of every mountain and the joyful coursing of every new river. And, because they were eternal, they had sung the works of Bach, Beethoven and Mozart long before those composers were even born. They thought they knew it all. But there was still one secret they didn't know.

[*Enter* GABRIEL]

One day, during a break in rehearsal, the Angel Gabriel suddenly appeared before them, and said:

GABRIEL
Ladies and Gentlemen! I want you to prepare for the biggest gig you will ever have done, in the most important place, for the most important audience ever, in the history of all Creation.

CHOIR
Ooooh!

CHOIRMASTER
The most important place? Is it the Concertgebouw?

CHORISTER 1
Is it Carnegie Hall?

CHORISTER 2
Is it the O2 Centre?

GABRIEL
Well, no. Actually it's a stable round the back of a pub, in a little town called Bethlehem.

CHOIR
Uuuuuh.

CHOIRMASTER
Bethlehem? What's so important about Bethlehem?

GABRIEL
Trust me, I'm an archangel. Here's your music. Keep up the good work! I've got to go and tell someone she's going to have a baby. [Exit]

CHOIRMASTER
That guy has really got to learn how to delegate. OK, people, let's give it a try!

NARRATOR
So the choir started rehearsing the music they'd been given for the special gig...

The Choir runs through the chorus of 'The Snow lay on the Ground'.
[*Enter* GABRIEL *with* Children's Choir]

NARRATOR (Cont.)
... And, as the concert drew nearer, Gabriel came back to see how they were getting on.

GABRIEL
How's it going, folks?

CHOIRMASTER
Oh, we'll be fine! This is really exciting! Bethlehem! That means it's a private VIP performance, right? No publicity. OK, we get it. So who's the audience?

GABRIEL
Well, there's a young couple with a new-born baby... Three fortune-tellers... Some local farm-workers... And some live-stock.

CHOIR
Errrr?

CHORISTER 1
Animals?

GABRIEL
Oh, I nearly forgot. You'll be performing with these cherubs.

CHORISTER 2
Animals *AND* children?

GABRIEL
Not long now! Keep up the good work. I've got to go and put up a new star in the east. [*Exit*]

CHOIRMASTER
Gabriel! Ever heard of outsourcing?

NARRATOR
So the Choir carried on rehearsing with the cherubs...
The Choir and the children's choir run through the chorus of 'The Snow lay on the Ground', while the Star takes up its position over the set.

NARRATOR (Cont.)
...Until finally the big day arrived, and once again the angel Gabriel came to pay them a visit.

GABRIEL
Well, here we all are in Bethlehem! The star's in place, the audience are on their way. We're all set for the biggest gig there ever was or ever will be!

CHOIRMASTER
Look, Gabriel, I don't understand. This the Heavenly Choir you're talking to! We're used to performing for God!

GABRIEL
Well... I'm not really supposed to tell you this... but God will be there...

CHOIR
Oooooh!

GABRIEL
...Only, sort of, in disguise.

CHOIR
Ohhhh!

GABRIEL
So this had better be good! Curtain up! It's time for your opening number. I've got to go and talk to some shepherds. [*Exit*]

CHOIRMASTER
Micromanagement, Gabriel! That archangel's heading for burn-out. OK, guys, here we go.
The Choir and the Children's Choir perform 'The Snow lay on the Ground' in full, while Mary and Joseph take their places with the Baby Jesus, then the three Wise Men follow the Star and kneel before the crib stage left, then Gabriel leads the shepherds and animals in and they kneel stage right.

CHOIRMASTER
Gabriel, who *are* these people?

1st WISE MAN
We are wise men from the East.

1st SHEPHERD
And we are shepherds.

1st WISE MAN
I've brought gold as a gift for the new king.

2nd WISE MAN
And I've brought frankincense.

3rd WISE MAN
And I've brought myrrh.

1st SHEPHERD
And we've brought some sheep.

CHOIRMASTER
But, Gabriel, you said God would be here! Which one is He?

GABRIEL
Well, if you look at the second piece of music I gave you, that might give you a clue.

CHOIRMASTER (quickly skims through the score of 'Away in a Manger')
Wow! It's the baby!

CHOIR
Aaaaah!

CHOIRMASTER

God has come to us as a child, and these people have brought whatever they have to honour Him. But all we have is our voices. So let's use them. Choir? Cherubs? Ready?

Choir and Children's Choir perform 'Away in a Manger'.

NARRATOR

After that, all the music they'd learnt made a lot more sense to the Heavenly Choir, and they sang for Jesus as they had never sung before. For now they understood what Creation was all about, and how one moment in time can change Eternity. They are singing now and forever, here and everywhere God's people are gathered and sing to His glory. But Gabriel never did learn how to delegate. Happy Christmas everyone!

THE END

Is This Your Sheep?

Dramatis personae:
Narrator
Jacob, Nathan, Reuben: Three shepherds
Melchior, Balthazar, Caspar: Three kings
The Angel Gabriel
Skipper the sheep
Joseph
Mary

Scene I
Reuben, Jacob, Nathan, Skipper, Gabriel

[The congregation sings While Shepherds Watched, and the cast take their first positions during the last verse. Jacob, Nathan and Reuben stand up and wave as the Narrator introduces them. They and Skipper then act out the Narrator's description of events.]

Narrator: Once upon a time, in the scrubby, rolling hills of Old Judaea, there were three shepherds - Jacob and Nathan, and their little brother, Reuben. They had a manageable, medium-sized flock of contented, well-behaved sheep, they were never bothered by wolves or bears, and although Jacob and Nathan did their best to teach Reuben all the ins and outs of good shepherding, there really wasn't very much for him to do. Then, one spring, one of the ewes had a particularly frisky little lamb.

Skipper: Baaa!

Narrator: So frisky, in fact, that as soon as he could stand up he started jumping, and as soon as he could walk he started trying to run away. It was almost a full time job just keeping him in the flock. But he was a very sweet and pretty little lamb, so Jacob and Nathan called him Skipper, and gave him to Reuben to look after.

Jacob: This is your job, now, Reuben. You make sure Skipper doesn't run away.

Rueben: I'll do my best!

Narrator: After that, Reuben spent quite a lot of his time running around, chasing after Skipper, but it was good fun, and he was happy to have a proper job at last.
But that winter, when Skipper was about eight months old, a very strange thing happened. It was a brightly moon-lit night. All the sheep, even the frisky ones, were dozing on the grass, and the three shepherds were sitting around their fire, when suddenly there was a flash of golden light, and an angel appeared in the sky above them.

Gabriel: Don't be afraid, shepherds! I am the angel Gabriel, and I've come to give you some wonderful news! The long night is over, and God himself has come among you as a new-born baby! He will grow up to be the greatest shepherd of all, and save everyone who follows him from wickedness and death. So stop what you're doing, get up and go to Bethlehem. You will find Mary and Joseph and the baby in a stable behind an inn. He will be lying in a manger, and there you can be among the first to worship him, the new-born king of all creation!

Narrator: And with that, the angel disappeared. The shepherds were very excited.

Jacob: I've never seen an angel before!

Nathan: Neither have I! We'd better do as he says. Which way is Bethlehem?

Jacob: It's over there. But hang on - what about the sheep?

Nathan: They'll be all right, at least...

Narrator: And then they realised there was a problem.

Jacob: Reuben, we can't take Skipper with us. You're going to have to stay behind and make sure he doesn't run away.

Reuben: But that's not fair!

Nathan: Sorry, Reuben. Somebody has to look after the sheep. It's a very important job! And when we get to Bethlehem we'll make sure we do some extra worshipping, just for you. Come on, Jacob!

Narrator: And off they went, into the night. Reuben was very unhappy.

[Skipper wakes up, sneaks away and disappears]

Reuben: This is all wrong! That angel was talking to me as well! And *I* want to go and worship the new king! In person! And I can't! All because I have to stay and watch out for Skipper... *[He looks around]* Skipper? Skipper! Oh, no! *[He runs off, calling for Skipper]*

Scene II

Reuben, Caspar, Skipper

Narrator: So Reuben ran into the hills, criss-crossing the paths between Skipper's favourite playgrounds, when suddenly he saw an old traveller in very fancy clothes, looking very important and very lost, and very puzzled.

[Skipper is revealed, hanging on to Caspar's leg]

Caspar: Hello! You look like a shepherd boy. Er... Is this your sheep?

Reuben: Yes! Oh, thank you, sir! How did you find him?

Caspar: Actually, he found me. Do you know this country well?

Reuben: Every inch of it, sir. Why, are you lost?

Caspar: Well, I'm supposed to be following that star, so that I can find a new-born king and worship him. I've come a long way, and I've even brought some gold as a gift. But the road twists and turns, and I'm afraid to leave it.

[Skipper runs away again]

Reuben: You're going to Bethlehem! My brothers have gone there too, but I had to stay behind and look after... my sheep! He's gone again!

Caspar: He's over there, under the star! I'll follow you.

Scene III

Reuben, Caspar, Melchior, Balthazar, Skipper

Narrator: So off they went, over the hills, across the paths, chasing after Reuben's sheep, until they found themselves running up to two more travellers in very fancy clothes, looking very important, and very lost, and very puzzled.

[Skipper is revealed hanging on to Balthazar's leg]

Balthazar: Melchior, this gentleman has a most regal appearance. He's clearly one of us. But his companion looks like a shepherd boy. *[to Reuben]* Er... Is this your sheep?

Reuben: Yes! Oh, thank you, sir! How did you find him?

Balthazar: Actually he found us. Do you know this country well? *[Skipper sneaks off again]* We're supposed to be following that star, so that we can find a new-born king and worship him. We've come a long way, and we've even brought some myrrh and some frankincense as gifts, but the road twists and turns and we're afraid to leave it.

Caspar: Don't worry, gentlemen. I'm on the same journey, and I was getting lost as well. But this boy knows every inch of the land. His brothers have also gone to worship the new king, but he had to stay behind to look after...

Reuben: My sheep! He's gone again!

Balthazar: He's over there, under the star! Go on, we'll follow you.

Scene IV

Reuben, Caspar, Melchior, Balthazar, Jacob, Nathan, Joseph, Mary, Skipper

Narrator: So Reuben chased after Skipper, and the three mysterious travellers chased after Reuben, across the paths and over the hills, until they found themselves on the outskirts of a little town. Reuben couldn't see Skipper any more, and he started turning corners at random, getting more and more anxious as he went, until suddenly he came to a stable at the back of an inn, and there were his brothers standing there, looking sheepish.

Nathan: Reuben! What are you doing here?

Jacob: You're supposed to be looking after Skipper!

[The three Wise Men catch up, panting]

Reuben: I was looking after him, but he ran away and led me to these royal gentlemen, and then all the way to Bethlehem. They have also come to worship the new king, and they've brought expensive gifts all the way from their own countries. Look: gold, frankincense, and myrrh.

Nathan: Oh, no! That's why we're standing out here. We didn't bring any gifts, and we're too shy to go in.

Jacob: We left in such a hurry, we didn't think about it. What are we going to do?

Narrator: But just then the door of the stable opened, and out came a man who looked very tired, very happy, but also a little puzzled. And that's when Reuben remembered what the angel Gabriel had said, and had the best and brightest idea of his young life.

[Enter Joseph. Skipper is revealed hanging on to him.]

Reuben: Er... Is your name Joseph?

Joseph: Yes. Er... Is this your sheep?

Reuben: Well, I've looked after him ever since he was little, and I followed him all the way here... But no, he's not my sheep. He's yours, for the baby, because the baby's going to be the greatest shepherd of all.

Joseph: What a wonderful gift! You'd all better come in, out of the cold.

All, *including Gabriel, form into a traditional Nativity scene around Mary and the crib, as the congregation sings* In The Bleak Midwinter.

THE END

A Birth Away from Home

Dramatis personae
Narrator
Joseph
Mary
Angel Gabriel
Innkeeper
Shepherds
Magi etc.

NARRATOR:
Spring is the time when all the world feels new,
And young creation sings its praise to God.
It's when the angels like to visit earth,
And on a day in spring, long, long ago,
When lambs were skipping in the fields around,
The Angel Gabriel from heaven came
To Nazareth, a town in Galilee,
Home of a girl engaged to be a bride,
To find her and appear to her alone.
Her name was Mary. She was scared at first,
And wondered what this vision meant for her.
But then the angel spoke, and calmed her fears.

GABRIEL:
Don't be afraid, Mary. I have great news.
Tell Joseph that his love for you is blessed.
Of all your sex the Lord has chosen you
To be the channel of his Providence.
You're going to have a baby who will be
The Holy one of God, the King of All.
Emmanuel, or Jesus, he'll be called,
And he will take his forebear David's throne,
Rule Jacob's people in his majesty,
And of his kingdom there shall be no end.
Six months ago your cousin, too, conceived,
So her son can prepare the way for yours.
Go to her now, and see my prophecy
Confirmed in joyful kicks inside her womb.
All hail to you, most highly favoured Maid!
Angels and men shall bow before your name.

MARY:
I will be brave, and do just as I'm told.
I am a faithful servant of the Lord.
What He ordains, so let it be with me.

NARRATOR:
Well said, young girl. And, so the days went by.
Elisabeth, her cousin, welcomed her,
And John, the forming child, leapt at her voice.
She stayed to see him born, then travelled home,
Knowing she had just half a year to wait
Before the angel's words would be fulfilled.
But then, just as her time was nearly come,
And all arrangements for the birth were made,
Caesar Augustus issued a decree
That all the world should pay him what it owed,

And every man should register his name
And lineage wherever he was born.
For Joseph that meant Bethlehem, and so
One cold and windy day they saddled up,
And made their way along the bumpy road.

JOSEPH:
The angel didn't tell you about this!
I thought you'd have your baby in your home
With friends and family to hold your hand!

MARY:
I am a faithful servant of the Lord.
What he ordains, so let it be with me.

NARRATOR:
The road was steep and winding through the hills,
And when at last they got to Bethlehem
The streets were full of travellers like them,
Dusty and tired and muttering with rage
At being forced to leave their cosy homes
To satisfy the Roman treasury.
But worse than that, because they were so late,
They found that all the rooms in town were booked.
The door of every boarding house was closed;
The grand hotels were only selling wine.
Only a lowly inn might have some space,
And so, with sinking heart, Joseph approached.

JOSEPH:
No family, no friends, now no hotel.
What kind of man could treat a girl that way?

MARY:
I am a faithful servant of the Lord.
What He ordains, so let it be with me.

[*JOSEPH knocks on the inn door*]

INN-KEEPER:
You looking for a room? I'm sorry, friends,
My inn's full up. You'll have to look elsewhere.

JOSEPH:
But can't you see we're going to have a child?
Already we're alone without a friend,
No family, no midwife for support.
There's nowhere left in town! We're desperate!

INN-KEEPER:
But you don't want to have your baby here!
The place is packed with drinking songs and fights,
Family squabbles dragged from far away.
I've got a little stable round the back.
It's not a palace, but at least it's warm.
My beasts are welcoming and innocent,
Birthing and tending young is all they know.
If angels came, that's where they'd want to stay.

JOSEPH:
So not even a bed. Well, thank you, sir.
Come on, my love. We'll do the best we can.

MARY:
I am a faithful servant...

JOSEPH:
Yes, I know.

NARRATOR:
They settled in the stable with the beasts.
But Gabriel was watching from above,
And, looking round the countryside, he saw
Three shepherds, and appeared to them at once.

GABRIEL:
Don't be afraid, you shepherds! Listen up!
Tonight in David's city there is born
The greatest shepherd there will ever be,
Greater than David, and a greater King.
Your Saviour, Christ the Lord, commands that you,
His family, attend with love and prayers.
Kings there will be as well, drawn by the star
That shines above the stable where he lies,
With costly gifts symbolic of his fate.
That's not your job. Just be there, and adore.

NARRATOR:
He vanished, and they gathered up their wits.

FIRST SHEPHERD:
The Holy One calls us his family?
And we must kneel with kings to worship him?
We can't be late! We'd better go at once!

NARRATOR

As glory flared around them, off they ran.
Finding the stable and the star above,
They knelt before the mother and her child,
Exalted in their wonder and their faith.
And then, behind them, creeping and afraid,
The king philosophers came with their gifts,
Humbled and prone before divinity.
Then all was still. The Lord of Life was born,
God was made man. And now the angels came.

THE END

www.ingramcontent.com/pod-product-compliance
Lightning Source LLC
Chambersburg PA
CBHW071325080526
44587CB00018B/3348